Total Woman

Total Woman

VIRTUOUS

JACQUELINE DUNCOMBE

Total Woman

Copyright © 2019 by Jacqueline Duncombe. All rights reserved.

No part of this publication may be reproduced, stored in a retrieval system or transmitted in any way by any means, electronic, mechanical, photocopy, recording or otherwise without the prior permission of the author except as provided by USA copyright law.

The opinions expressed by the author are not necessarily those of URLink Print and Media.

1603 Capitol Ave., Suite 310 Cheyenne, Wyoming USA 82001
1-888-980-6523 | admin@urlinkpublishing.com

URLink Print and Media is committed to excellence in the publishing industry.

Book design copyright © 2019 by URLink Print and Media. All rights reserved.

Published in the United States of America
ISBN 978-1-64753-000-6 (Paperback)
ISBN 978-1-64367-995-2 (Digital)

15.10.19

DEDICATION

This book is dedicated to all my sisters in Christ. I pray that this study will shed some light on a situation you may encounter and also, help you in your Christian walk. This book is not to condemn anyone, but it was written under the guidance of our Lord Jesus Christ that it may strengthen ladies in the weak areas. (The word of God says, "Iron sharpens iron.") This book is Bible based with the scriptures listed for easy reference. May you be blessed as you read.

For too long Christians were afraid to speak openly about life and its ordeals, this book speaks openly about issues that Christian women face daily. This is REAL Talk.

CONTENTS

Introduction 9
Singleness 11
Divorced 15
Entrepreneur 17
Operate Your Business With Integrity 19
Appearance 20
The Mate 23
Dating 27
Formal Dinning 33
Marriage 34
Unsaved Husband 39
Order 40
Sexual Needs 42
Keep The Intimacy In Your Marriage 44
Faithfulness In Relationship 45
Conclusion 49

INTRODUCTION

TOTAL WOMAN

(PROVERBS 31:10)

"WHO CAN FIND A VIRTUOUS WOMAN? FOR HER PRICE IS FAR ABOVE RUBIES."

"HER CHILDREN ARISE UP, AND CALL HER BLESSED; HER HUSBAND ALSO, AND HE PRAISETH HER."

"GIVE HER OF THE FRUIT OF HER HANDS; AND LET HER OWN WORKS PRAISE HER IN THE GATES."

Who is a virtuous woman?

A virtuous woman is:

1. A working woman (not idle/lazy)/Entrepreneur
2. Strong/(spiritually/emotionally)
3. Kind/unselfish-gives of herself
4. Not broke
5. Eat properly & exercise; takes care of her body/mind.

6. Has faith in God.
7. Lives a holy life.
8. Has disciplined children/Takes care of her home.

Do you have to be married to be virtuous?
A virtuous woman can be either single or married.

SINGLENESS

Most women would like to be married at some time or other in their lives, the reason being because you were made to be 'completed' by a man. (1Corinthians 11-9). If you say you do not want a man right now that is understood. Some women say God is their husband, He will protect you, provide for you etc. like a husband but God is spirit and he will not jump into bed with you at right when you need to be held or sexually fulfilled.

Homosexuality is an abomination in the sight of God. Two of the same sex can probably give each other a good feeling but it ends there, they cannot produce. God is a God of reproduction (... be fruitful and multiply). As a Christian woman if you are fighting that demonic spirit you need that demon cast out of you immediately.

To become a virtuous woman, we first have to accept the free gift of salvation, an unsaved woman can have good morals, but to be virtuous you must be Christ like. Upon accepting the Lord as your personal Saviour your next step is living holy. People are going to remind you from whence you came, but remember II Corinthians 5=7 "Therefore if any man be in Christ he is a new creature, old things are passed away, behold all things become new." You will not be perfect, but if you slip up, don't give up, get back in the race. Be women of integrity, pay your bills, if you don't have the money this month call the creditor and reason with them. Do not have your children and family members lying for you – dodging. (Proverbs 19=1). A lot of times it looks like the unsaved people are prospering and are able to pay their bills on time, but remember the word of God Psalms 37=7 "Fret not thyself because of him who proper in his way."

You don't know what they are doing to prosper, so don't get jealous or envious. Hold the faith and live holy. To live holy you have to abstain from gossiping, tearing down people, lying, malice, hatred, unfaithfulness, doubting God, take on the fruits of the spirit. Study Matthew 5 – The Beatitudes, this is the type of attitude we should possess.

Too many Christian women suffer from low self-esteem or no self-esteem. Be proud of who you are: you were fearfully and wonderfully made. When you are confident of who you are then you will be able to compliment another woman sincerely. Be your sister's keeper. Stop being envious of each other. Stop tearing down each other. If you cannot give constructive criticism, don't give any at all. If it is not of a good report don't think about it. (Philippians 4=8) Constantly lift your sisters up in prayer.

One of the most common hidden sins young single Christian women commit is fornication. Everyone wants a man and it seems they will do whatever it takes to get one. (1Peter 2=11 & 1Corinthians 6=15-17.) There is a term for sex, "function at the junction" but the only junction you need to function at is the junction between life and death, heaven or hell. During sex the man leaves a spirit in you. Don't be fooled ladies, oral sex is fornication as well. If you never knew how to pray it's time you learn. (1Corinthians 6=13, 18-20) A single woman's first priority is to God. How she may please Him. She should be Holy both in body and spirit." ... for when they have begun to wax wanton against Christ, then will they marry." (1Timothy 5=11) She should be in church every time the doors open for service. (1Corinthians 7=32)

If you are faithful to God, He is faithful that promise. He is not man that He should lie; God's word cannot return to Him void it must accomplish which He has sent it out to do; just serve God with your whole heart. Ruth was faithful to God (Ruth 1=16) and He sent her a mighty man of wealth for a husband and blessed their marriage with a son. (Ruth 4=13)

When you are unfaithful, service is going on and you stay at home when you should be in church. ".... They learn to be idle, tattlers, busybodies speaking and doing things they ought not." Satan sends trouble your way. Trouble is easy to get into but very hard to get out. Christian single women I entreat you, *keep your legs closed, and also, leave people's business alone.* (1Thessalonians 4=3) Let us bring the men up to our standard. If a young man is interested in you, let him know *no ring, no thing*. Every guy in church is not a saint. The devil goes to church as well. When you fornicate all you are doing is wearing out your body, by the time God sends your husband your body is worn and tired; therefore, when your husband gets the urge to merge you turn your back or you have a headache, night after night it's a different ache. So, you sex starve your husband and yourself, because your body is worn out from the premarital activities. What happens next, Satan sends Jane Dow along, she may not be as fine as you are but she is willing to function at the junction whenever, your man wants. Then we talk about him saying his wife looks 100% better than Jane Dow, not knowing the story. (Believe me I am totally against adultery) But 1Timothy 5=14 says leave not room to the enemy. If he decides to walk out of the relationship, just ensure that you have done your part. For the new converts you need a spiritual mother who hears from God, so when you are operating in the flesh she can be in the spirit praying and giving you Godly council.

DIVORCED

If you are single because of divorce and you find yourself at a crossroad in your life and you don't know how to go on begin from where you are now, take one day at a time, don't wallow in self-pity. Do not allow yourself to become bitter but purpose in yourself to become better. You shall not be called 'Mira'. The divorce was an event, but the healing is a process. Before you get involved in another relationship, or before you start to think about dating, spend some time in the presence of God and allow Him to take you through your healing process. Give yourself time to heal and room to grow. If you do not heal you will carry old baggage into the new relationship and it could destroy both you and your partner.

"How long should you allow yourself to heal?" That depends on how deep is your hurt. Sometimes it is not realized how deeply rooted the pain is, until the healing process has started. Do not allow yourself to be pitiful, shameful or prideful. Take responsibility for your actions. 'Forgetting those things that are behind, press toward the mark of the prize of a higher calling which is in Christ Jesus.' Remember the word of God says, 'old things are pass away and behold all things have become new.' Walk in grace and let the fruits of the spirit be manifested in your life daily. (Gal. 5=22)

When you and your ex-spouse can sit down and have a meaningful conversation without it ending with insults or if you see him and your heart does not tighten for whatever reason, love/hate/anger etc. When you can love him with the love of God (agape love) in spite of his faults and what he has done to you. You are well on your way in your healing process.

I therefore, beseech you, ensure that you are totally healed and delivered from the spirits of your past before you consider walking down the aisle again.

ENTREPRENEUR

Who is an Entrepreneur?

An entrepreneur is someone who organizes his or her own business and assumes the risk of that business.

God has given each person a gift and a measure of faith. In the Parable of the talents each man was given a different amount of talents to utilize. The one that hid his talent got it taken away from him but the others who put his to use, it multiplied. (Matthew 25=14-30)

If you do not know what your gift is, ask God to reveal to you your creative side. My Pastor once told me of an old Chinese proverb, 'turn your adversity into opportunity'. (Example: If you like to eat open a food store/restaurant.) Do not waste your talent. We do not need another business in the country that's ordinary – don't be afraid to be different – it sells. If God has put something in your spirits, do not procrastinate; step out on faith – start small if you must, but start. If God has given you a vision. He will make provision. "Your faith should not stand in the wisdom of men, but in the power of God."

Operate your business with integrity, give quality service with a good attitude and a friendly smile. Remember that your customers should be catered to, the best customer is a repeat customer. Treat your employees as assets – team work, will make the dream work. Kingdomites should be employers and not employees, above and not beneath. The lenders and not the borrowers.

OPERATE YOUR BUSINESS WITH INTEGRITY

APPEARANCE

A virtuous woman also takes pride in her appearance. I feel that low self-esteem has a lot to do with the way we carry ourselves. Women, remember because we are saints does not mean we are exempted from smelling. If we don't bathe, use deodorant and brush our teeth every day we will smell. We cannot get too saved until we neglect personal hygiene. We need at least the basics, I call it the Daily Three (3).

   i. Brush your teeth and tongue – avoid halitosis
   ii. Take a bath and comb your hair daily (your hair is your glory – 1Corinthian 11=15
   iii. Wear deodorant

A lot of people are allergic to perfume and some women don't like make-up so these are optional: make sure moisturize your face so it would not look ashy/dry. Keep your finger and toe nails clean and filed neatly. Polish is optional.

Those areas on your body where there is excessive hair keep the hair shaved or trimmed neatly because hair carries odor when you sweat, and we live in a tropical climate (e.g. Arm pits, etc.).

TOTAL WOMAN

The Bible says body exercise profit little. Exercise at least three times a week. You do not have to become a member of a Fitness Club (gym), but at least walk around the block of your neighborhood or do some other type of work-out for about twenty minutes every other day.

When Esther was about to go before the king she prepared herself for one year in advance. (Esther 2 = 12). So, you single women believing God for a husband, use this time for preparation. Get rid of some of those debts; purchase a piece of property (land), get your own car, don't look so needy; be independent. Fix up yourself. Wear the right size clothing, some people know that they are a size 13, but yet they buy a size 10. It is not attractive at all. (1Timothy 2=9) Women learn to dress appropriately, wear the right underwear with your clothing. Your clothing does not have to be a name brand or expensive but make sure they are in good taste. One suggestion: purchase fabric and have your outfits made.

I would not tell you what to wear and the length but pray and ask the Lord's guidance in this area and anytime you put on something contrary, the Holy Ghost will convict you. Single women always remember that the way you carry yourself is the type of men you will attract. Example: if you are a lady of class then you will attract men of class. (If you want to be address properly, then dress properly.) 'If we are really Saints of the Most High God, let us dress that way, with good taste and style and the freedom to wear the colours of God's rainbow; but never be afraid to be the woman God made.' Ladies, every new fashion that comes on the market is not for kingdom women, discern which fashion is for you. Maybe you can design your own clothing, who knows, where this gift may take you... perhaps your own label. Don't blend in, stand out.

Instead of wearing short pants or tights with a big T-shirt to bed wear nightgowns or pajamas. Do not go to bed 'whole sale'. If you must tie your hair, use a nice scarf or stain cap, please ladies no old stocking or piece of 'tear up' cloth. Start taking good care of yourself now, when you get married it will be a life style. Take time with your appearance, when you look good, you feel good, your self-esteem rises and we will not be envious of the sister who looks good, but you can genuinely compliment her on her appearance. Let's work on the inside as well as the outside – Wholeness. The outside will attract the mate but the inside (attitude) will attach the mate.

THE MATE

After you have allowed God to work on you by making and molding you into His image and likeness, take on the character of God, your self-esteem is what it should be and you are satisfied with your singleness, then, you are ready for a mate.

Your first step in this process is to seek God's guidance. Talk to God, be specific in your prayer concerning the characteristics you would like in your mate. Then, what do you do next: stand, until God sends the man. Do not go out looking for 'no' man. God does not need your help. A woman does not marry a man. Man marries woman (Proverbs 18=22).

While you are waiting, Satan will send counterfeits your way to sidetrack you. Sisters don't be fooled. Remember when you prayed to God about your mate Satan heard your prayer as well. So of cause he sends this fine specimen in your path. "Guess who?" "The devil that's who." Your first question to him, "Are you saved?" "No?" "Speak to the hand, the face is not listening." If you marry an unsaved man you are in open rebellion against God. (II Corinthians 6=14) If you sin in the face of knowledge then you will receive the judgement of God, which can be in any form (death, sickness, problems etc.). After the judgement then you receive peace because of God's mercy (Deuteronomy 7=3-4). Tell that unsaved brother to keep on keeping on, you are a Princess of God. Your next question to him if he is saved "Do you have a job?" you do not need an unstable man in your life who cannot keep a job. I am sure you do not need help to do bad, that, you can do all yourself.

When the 'saved' brother in the church comes along with his Bible under his arm, if he wants to come to your house for Bible study tell him meet you at the library or invite a few others over as well and make sure he leaves when they do. Maybe he wants to take you out for dinner or ice-cream, you know they like to invite themselves in for a cup of tea/coffee afterwards the devil is a liar, one cup of tea/coffee could last all night long. Sometimes men can tell if you have not had sex in a long time because you look so wanton and desperate. Act cool, keep that flesh under control.

When the married man comes along, with his story, send him to his Pastor along with his wife for counseling, you are not a marriage counselor. Ladies if you are believing God for a particular man and he is married, if you are praying for his wife to die or for him to leave her – stop letting the devil use you, seek God for your own husband. This is where your spiritual mother comes in, she could rebuke you and put you back on track.

When God sends *thee one, come on say it out loud, 'thee one'* you will know, you do not need someone to prophesy to you, to tell you who your husband is, just stay connected to God and the word through the Prophet will come as confirmation. (I Corinthian 13=9) He may be lacking one or two of the characteristics you prayed for, don't despair sometimes God gives us an apple seed instead of an apple tree; we have to plant and water the tree and allow it to grow into a nice apple tree. Some characteristics of a good husband are: - he watches out for what lies ahead, a man with vision, keeps his commitments and his responsibility to God, his wife and children and he is also a good provider.

(Example) You may have prayed for a rich man, but Joe Doe may not have riches yet, but he could be headed for riches. "She that is spiritual judgeth all things."

Another case, the Lord told you a particular man is your husband, you are positive it was God and not the flesh; but this man is not saved or delivered; what do you do? Leave that man alone and allow God to work on him. When God has done a complete work on him, (if it was, in fact, God the Father and not God of the flesh that spoke to you,) He will send him back into your life.

We so often like to remind God of (Psalm 3=4 Lord you promise to grant me the desires of my heart). But if God has a special purpose for you He will change the desire of your heart to become the desire of his heart and He will not be a liar because it is now the desire of your heart.

One advice, wait on the Lord and be of good courage. Remember ladies God's choice for us is not always mummy's choice for us. "Who will you obey?" 'Soulish ties' has no place in the kingdom of God, we have to break those ties that bind us and try to exalt itself above God.

The Lord will not give you anything that will destroy you or take you away from him. If your earthly father knows how to give good gifts, what more do you think about your heavenly Father? "It is written, eye hath not seen, nor ear heard, neither have entered into the heart of man, the things which God hath prepared for them that love him."

DATING

How does a Christian couple date?

The Bible does not give us guidelines on how to date, it only instructs us on marriage. One suggestion is double date with other couples until you know the individual quite well. If you live alone do not invite him to your home; or if he lives alone do not go to his place by yourself, if he invites you over, take a 'Spiritual' girlfriend with you.

Why should you not go to his place alone?

- ❖ It is not proper.
- ❖ Give no room to the enemy.

When dating, you may hold hands but avoid fore play – French kissing, fondling, necking, these are preparations for sex and you do not need to arouse your feelings. Maybe you think you can do one of the above and stay in control of yourself, even if you can, you should be sensitive to your date's feelings. As a matter of fact you should not want to defile your temple (body).

How long should I date?

We have no instructions from the Bible on the length of time to date, it depends on the individuals. Jacob waited for Rachel for fourteen years (Genesis 29=28); but in my opinion if you are certain this relationship is of God, you don't have to date for years. This is how you get into trouble because you already see this man as your husband, especially if you are doing things for him: - washing, cooking, ironing etc. – the next step will be **Sex.** Saved, love the Lord but having sex.

In my humble opinion, I feel a year and a half (Eighteen months to two years is long enough time – the pretending should be over by then. It is a known fact that in new relationships most persons do not show their "real self" until after three or four months but I suggest that you let the Lord lead you.

I advise you though, to use this period to get to know him, personality. Habits, likes and dislikes. Ensure that this is the man for you. Make sure that he is "above board" don't take anything that the Lord shows you for granted. If you see negative traits, mental, physical, verbal abuse: manipulation, bad work ethics... address them. Run, don't take on the responsibility to change him; that's God's job. If you marry him knowing this, you have to ask yourself, "am I a victim or a volunteer?"

Do not marry out of the will of God. Remember that "until death do you part."

Some ideas of places to go: - movies (be selective with your movie choice), dinners, ball games, fairs, theatre, church services, picnics, visiting relatives and friends (see how he relates with your family and friends).

First Date Etiquette for Men and Women

A first date is all about first impressions and you want to make a good one. With all the pressure and nervousness we feel before a first date, it is not always easy to realize whether the things we do on a first date will leave a good or bad impression.

Do not give any false impressions about yourself. Whether the date works out or not, you should always be remembered as the person who was comfortable and delightful to spend some time with.

A first date should be at a place where the couple can sit and talk and have good eye contact with each other while getting to know more about each other.

What to do...

1. **Give a Confirmation Call (optional)**
   Giving a quick call to confirm your date will make you both feel relaxed and peaceful. It will prevent any misunderstandings or miscommunications and will also relieve any worries about you or date being stood up. Plus. It also shows how much you are actually looking forward to meeting your date. Do not appear over eager.

2. **Make Eye-Contact**
   Making eye contact on a date is very important. It makes the other person feel important and that you are actually interested and paying attention

to what he or she is saying. No eye contact could appear as rude or untrustworthy.

3. **Give Compliments**

    Be sure to give your date a nice compliment – whether it be on their hair, clothes, smile or whatever you personally notice. Giving compliments will show your date that you cared enough to take the time to observe the efforts they made in putting themselves together.

4. **Laugh at His/Her Jokes**

    Whether you truly think your date's jokes and sense of humor is actually funny, it is always polite to give a laugh. To laugh at his/her jokes and humor will show the appreciation you have for the efforts they made to make the date interesting. So give him/her a laugh, without being over the top or making it look fake or forced.

5. **Questions to ask**

    You can ask questions to your date about their work, hobbies, church they attend, whether or not they are a Christian, and so on, or just ask the person to tell you about themselves.

    Do not be too direct and forward with your questions, do not appear as if you are drilling, although you may want too, or badgering the person. Use conversational voice and when necessary speak with a smile in your voice.

    Do not ask their yearly income, marriage plans and so on. You do not need to introduce them to your Pastor, Parents or children just yet. Remember, this is a first date: do not scare your date away with a 'too much too soon' impression.

6. **Who pays for the date?**
   In today's world women are now very liberated and demand equal rights, so to this end, the person who extended the invitation for the date; should be the person to pay, unless otherwise arranged by the couple. But since this is the first date and you were invited by the man, he should pay.

7. **Getting to the date**
   If you can help it, do not allow the date to pick you up, arrange to meet at the venue. If the date is picking you up; here are some things you should carry in your bag; - enough money to pay for your meal and catch a cab in case the date goes wrong. A pen and paper should you need to write the car license plate number down or any important information. If you have a cell phone take it with you and ensure that you have minutes and that the battery is charged. Take a small pepper spray or a small bottle of cologne to spray in the eyes of a predator. You may not need to use these items but it is good to be prepared. Old proverb, better to have and not need, than to need and not have.

What not to do....

1. **Do not talk on the Phone**
   Nothing is ruder than talking on your cell phone during your date, or checking messages constantly while on a date. It expresses not only rudeness, but that you may also be bored and uninterested in your date, making him/her feel insecure and upset. So wait until the end of your date to check messages and if you must keep your cell-phone on and answer it, then keep your talk short and

let the caller know that you are busy and will get back to them later.

2. **Do not be late**

    Being late for a date is more than just being late. It gives the impression that you do not respect your dates time and that you are also someone that cannot be relied on. Show your date that you value time and are responsible by showing up on time. This is a quality that everyone find attractive.

3. **Do not talk too closely**

    Do not make your date uncomfortable by getting too close to them when you talk. People need to feel like they still have their own personal space and if they suddenly feel suffocated, then they will close up and you will not be able to learn as much about them as you would like.

4. **Do not be too Aggressive or Direct**

    There is a difference in being flirty and being too aggressive. There is also a difference between asking questions to get to know your date better and just being too direct. If you like your date, feel free to flirt and have fun. You do not really know your date at this point, keep your flirting simple and set personal and silent boundaries.

5. **Do not get intimate**

    Do not be touchy feely and do not get sexy with your talk. Do not talk about intimate details such as body parts or sexual habits or conquers pass or present. Definitely no kissing or sex.

FORMAL DINNING

Ladies table manners is important. When God sends that man along and he takes you out to dinner, you need to know how to deport yourself.

1. Single ladies when your date picks you up, let him come to the door (NO HORN BLOWING) you do not live in the street.
2. Find out the restaurant ahead and dress appropriately.
3. Ladies let him open doors for you.
4. If you want to be treated like the princess that you are, act like one.
5. Know your table setup/ practice good posture/ display good table manners (If you are unsure about something, do not do it. Finger foods should be avoided in a formal restaurant.) Example: crabs
6. The napkin is for your lap and not around your neck – around the neck is for the toddlers.
7. After dinner you may touch up your lipstick at the table but I suggest that you use the restroom so you can use a mirror to do it properly and powder your nose as well. **YOUR SPOON IS NOT A MIRROR.**

DO NOT FUSS WITH YOUR HAIR AT THE TABLE.

MARRIAGE

For this cause shall a man leave his father and mother, and leave to his wife: and they two shall be one flesh: so then they are no more two, but one flesh. What therefore God has joined together let *no* man put asunder. (Mark 10=7-9)

A prudent wife is from the Lord. (Proverbs 19=14)

To avoid fornication let every husband have his own wife. (I Corinthians 7=2)

God ordained marriage. He ordained it for three reasons:

1. To illustrate the character of God (Trinity-Father, Son and Holy Ghost) / husband / wife / offspring.
2. Procreation (which is children) to replenish the earth
3. Man needs a helper, so he gave him a help-mate by his side. One man cannot do everything God wants done in the family. He is the head of the family team.

Marriage is a covenant made by God.
What is a covenant? A covenant is a formal binding agreement between two or more parties.

If you want God's blessings, then you have to function under God's laws. When you get married you cut a covenant with God and your spouse. The first marriage covenant took place in Genesis between God, Adam and Eve. (Genesis 2=22) God cut the marriage covenant with the shedding of blood. This is the reason when the hymen is broken blood is shed which also proves that sex is only ordained for marriage. In the Bible days, on a couple's wedding night the bride's father stood outside the tent while the couple consummates the marriage. After consummation, the husband would give the bloody sheets to the girl's father as a sign that she was a virgin and seals the covenant. If the bride was found not to be a virgin, the contract could become null and void, if the husband chooses to do so, and the girl would be stoned in the streets.

Marriage is serious business in the sight of God, so serious, that the prayers of a husband can be hindered if he mistreats his wife. The Bible admonishes men to love their wives and wives to submit unto their husbands. He should be your 'lord'. Sarah called Abraham lord because he loved her, provided for her and he treated her with respect. God recognizes all heterosexual (male & female) marriages. He may not have ordained all marriages, but he recognizes them all, both sinners and Christians. This is the reason why John the Baptist told Herod that it is wrong for him to have his Brother Philip's wife. If you have already committed this act, by marrying unequally yoke without knowing, ask God's forgiveness and as Jesus said to the woman caught in adultery go and sin no more.

The wife is to make the home comfortable for she is her husband's crowning glory. (I Corinthians 11=7) Keep your house clean, have the necessity in the house. Wash the clothes, cook the food and keep the children fed and clean.

A virtuous woman is a crown to her husband, but she that maketh ashamed is a rottenness in his bones. (Proverbs 12=4) A wife without discretion is like a pig wallowing in slop. Because it is God ordained does not mean you will not encounter challenges, but because God is the center you can work through those challenges. A couple who were celebrating their 50th Wedding Anniversary was asked the question, "How did you stayed married all those years, the wife answered, "we did not fall out of love at the same time." While one person is going through changes, the other one should be praying them through. This is why it is important to have a praying mate.

It is better to dwell on the housetop than to live in the house with a rowdy woman. You may get angry but please don't be a miserable person; rowing for everything and nothing. You will have differences especially in the beginning of the marriage because you are two persons with different upbringing and habits living together; there are going to be some days you just shut up and concede defeat. Put off all these: anger, wrath, malice, blasphemy, filthy communication out of your mouth and lie not one to another, seeing that ye have put off the old man with his deeds; and put on the new man which is renewed in knowledge after the image of God. (Col. 3=8-10) The word of God says "Submit one to another", both parties must submit to each other. Accept wrong for peace sake. Agree with your adversary quickly. A still tongue turns away wrath. Be ye angry and sin not, let not the sun go down upon your wrath, forbearing one another, and forgiving one another as Christ hath forgiven you. Let the peace of God rule in your hearts, to which also ye are called in one body.

Whosoever shall put away his wife and marry another commit adultery against her. And if a woman shall put away her husband, and be married to another, she commits adultery. Wives submit yourselves unto your own husbands as unto God. (Ephesians 5:22) If you are in a marriage and that man is physically abusing you; run for your life-today. Pray for his deliverance from a distance, you cannot change anyone let God change him. After he has been delivered, then you may go back. God only sanctioned divorce in the case of adultery. We have this notion about un-reconciled differences; separate until you reconcile your differences or remain separated. Divorce is not the antidote for every challenge you may face in a marriage.

In the case of **Physical death** – if your spouse dies you may remarry. There is no special length of time for mourning before you remarry, the old folks says six months to a year but this is a not Biblical it is just for 'decency'.

Spiritual death – if your mate dies to the covenant spiritually, backslide and is living unmorally, abusing you, you may divorce and remarry.

The husband is to love his wife as Christ love the Church and gave his life for it. Husbands love your wives and be not bitter against them. (Col. 3=19) "Enoch walked with God and he was not …." He was not broke, sick, lonely etc. because he and God were in agreement. Two cannot walk together except they agree. (I Corinthians 13=4&5) It will be easier to submit if love is shown, but even if love is not shown you still need to submit if you are going to be in the marriage and in the will of God. "He that doeth wrong shall receive for the wrong which he hath done: and there is no respect of persons." (Col. 3=25)

UNSAVED HUSBAND

Married women whose husbands are not saved if you got saved in the marriage do not leave your husband just because he is unsaved, because through your life living you can draw him to Christ. But if he wants to leave because he cannot handle being married to a Christian, then let him go. If he remains in the marriage, do not pressure him to get save, keep praying for his salvation and show him love that he will be convinced that this Christian *thing* is worth trying. Don't force him out, win him over. A lot of Christian women whose husbands are unsaved think that they are too holy for their husbands to touch them. Ladies give that man what he wants. (Remember you can have sex with your unsaved husband and still be saved.)

Women submit to your husbands, obey him. Obey your husband but not the devil in your husband. Satan will use him to get to you sometimes. A disobedient spirit is a serious spirit, when you want your husband and children to fall in place with the word of God, you need to line up with the word of God, 'line upon line, precept upon precept'. If you are in church or at work and operating in the spirit of disobedience, how you expect your children to be obedient to you; you reap what you sow. So, sow good seeds.

ORDER

The husband is the head of the home. God is behind the husband because he has put him in charge. So when the woman assumes the role of the head of the home with the man present, that house is out of order. The woman is out front alone without her covering. (She is on the front line in a war without back up.) She has left God and her husband behind because, remember, God is behind the husband. If you are uncovered you leave yourself open for more attacks from the enemy, the devil. (Example: children is disobedient or rebellious; your husband acting up, financial problems etc.) This is the reason ladies, you must marry right. Do not just go for good looks, riches, fancy cars or unequally yoked. The word of God says do not be unequally yoked with non-believers. But you can still be unequally yoked with a believer. For example: You may be an extravert and maybe he is an introvert; maybe you like to listen to a little love music every now and then but he is so spiritual that he thinks it's a sin. You may like to walk around the house in a little negligent and he thinks you need to put on some clothes before you catch a cold. For the bold woman, you need a man who can handle your boldness and don't feel threatened. Ladies, you don't need a husband who is so relax that you have to take control. If you have a husband like this, get him involved in everything and gently push him to the forefront of the home which is his rightful place, refer to the story of Judge Deborah a virtuous woman (Judges 4). Do not go against your husband's ruling made with the children or household. When your children comes to you for your approval let them know daddy has the final word. If you must, you can discuss things over with your spouse in private.

SEXUAL NEEDS

"Marriage is honorable in all and the bed undefiled. (Hebrew 13=4) A wife should not leave her husband's bed unless it is with consent, so ladies, before fasting talk it over with your husband. Your body does not belong to you anymore but to your husband and likewise the husband's to the wife. Your husband should not have to beg you for sex. As a matter of fact you are not to tell him **"no"** either, except in cases of illness. If you are not up to it (tired) explain to your husband and pray he understands. If not, ask him to give you a few minutes, go into the bath room take a nice shower/bath put on your sexiest underwear or night gown to get yourself in the mood then go back into bed.

Wives, if your husband likes a certain thing done to him in bed whether you like it or not do it. Please that man and make sure he pleases you. Wives its ok to ask your husband just to hold you, you don't want sex you just want to be held in the comfort of his strong arms. The bed is not the place to play cute, if you feel sexy, don't be bashful to initiate sex. The bed is the one place you can lead and still be in order. Sex plays an important part in your marriage. For the wife, it is rated about fifth on her list of things to do after taking care of the children, bills, house, but for the husband it is rated number one and everything else comes next. Wives if you are smart you will take care of that man's sexual needs first then present him with all the other situations you want him to handle. Watch the calendar, if you don't he probably would anyway, do not allow too much time to pass. Some women let weeks and months go by before making love with their husbands. You are looking for trouble. Keep the intimacy in your marriage.

KEEP THE INTIMACY IN YOUR MARRIAGE

FAITHFULNESS IN RELATIONSHIP

"Whoremongers and adulterers God will judge." (Hebrews 13=4)

If you suspect your husband is having an affair or is running around, use wisdom. Now if you have concrete evidence (not hear say) that your husband is committing adultery; first communicate with him and get to the root of the problem. Address the situation, please do not ignore it. Talk openly with your mate. If he continues to stay in the mess, you have permission in the word of God to separate. Separation can either come by sleeping in another bedroom or moving out of the house completely. If you continue to sleep with him unprotected you leave yourself open for sexually transmitted diseases. We have many Christian women dying from AIDS (Acquired Immune Deficiency Syndrome) in the church because of ignorance.

Ladies, we have women who have affairs on their husbands as well (the ratio is very high in save and unsaved women). This is the reason we have babies who don't look like anyone in the family and STD (Sexually Transmitted Diseases). When a man enters your body through intercourse and ejaculates into you, he leaves his spirit into you. This is the reason why you take on some of his character traits; or cannot get him out of your system (think about it.) "If you confess your sins, Christ is faithful and just to forgive you or your sins, and to cleanse you from all unrighteousness." For the women who have had sexual partners in the past and you are now believing God for a mate, I suggest you ask God to cleanse you and purge you to get rid of all those lurking spirits from the past. That goes for the married women who have had affairs also.

The word of God says, if a man looks at another woman to lust he has already committed adultery in his heart. You may not be committing physical adultery with a man and for the men a woman where you sleep with someone else while you are married to another, but maybe it is emotional adultery.

What is emotional adultery?

Some men/women have female/male "friends" that they are emotionally attached to and the chemistry between them is more than just a regular friend of the opposite sex; they confide in him/her, secretly go out together, can't wait to talk to him/her, misses him/her when he/she is not around or sulks when they cannot get to see him/her and they compare their mate with him/her. The grass always looks greener on the other side of the fence, but when you get on the other side you will find out that the grass over there needs moving also. No you have not slept with this individual.... yet. This is not a healthy relationship, you are committing emotional adultery. At the first sign of trouble between you and your mate you will probably sleep with this "friend". You need to cut off that relationship immediately, it's unhealthy... you are heading for trouble. When that man comes on to you, let him know from the get go, I am not interested. If you flirt with him you send the wrong signals. Yes women all want to feel attractive (or know that you still have it), if your mate does not tell you when you're looking good, go in front of the mirror and tell yourself – "girl you looking mighty fine today." So when the man on the street tells you, it's just confirmation. You say thank you politely and move on. He does not have to see your back teeth. The word on the street is that Christian women are '*hot*' (that include single, married, young and old women.) Women need to change the world's perception. The only thing on their minds is man, but it's the wrong man; keep Jesus Christ on your mind, pull down every vain imagination. Yes I am married, but I was not always married, I know about being Christian single lady but I had to put the flesh under subjection, turning down dates with guys, because my focus was on a higher prize. I implore you to crucify your flesh, because no good thing dwells in the flesh. After crucifixion comes resurrection. "Always bearing about in the body the dying of the Lord Jesus that the life also of Jesus might be made manifest in our body. For all things are for your sakes, that the abundant grace might through the thanksgiving of many redound to the glory of God. For our light affliction, which is but for a moment, worketh for us a far more exceeding and eternal weight of glory." (II Cor. 4 = 10, 15, 17)

CONCLUSION

Stay focus ladies, single, married or divorced. Whichever stage of the game of life you find yourself do not wait to live your life. Do not wait to start living when the bills are paid, when the children are grown, when the career is blooming etc. begin to live your bless and best days now. Good success is attainable, it is putting yourself where you see yourself – fulfilling your diving purpose.

Do not lose sight of the promise, God's word is true He only has good things in-store for you, delight yourself in Him and He will give you the desires of your heart. You have an adversary, the devil, he is like a roaring lion seeking whom he may devour; he cannot devour everyone, he can only devour those persons who are left without a hedge off protection around them (Job 1 = 10). Seeing you know these things before, beware lest you also, being led away with the error of the wicked fall from your own steadfastness. Be diligent that you may be found of Him in peace, without spot, and blameless. (II Peter 3 = 14, 17).

Grow in grace, and in the knowledge of our Lord and Saviour Jesus Christ; the race is not for the swiftest, but to those who endure to the end. *Blessings.*

www.ingramcontent.com/pod-product-compliance
Ingram Content Group UK Ltd.
Pitfield, Milton Keynes, MK11 3LW, UK
UKHW022218230426
12048UKWH00016BA/928